THE C CARD AND ME

How I beat Stage IV cancer (to a pulp)

by

Ali Gilmore

ISBN: 1470125501
ISBN- 9781470125509

Dedicated to my mom, Alice Gilmore, and the other fighters in my family who took up the sword before me; Jim Gilmore, Joel Duker, Laurie Gilmore, Leila Rie Serikaku-Takagi, Lisa Gilmore-Bell, Pat Friend, and Susan Kahn.

Prologue

❖ ❖ ❖

If you're reading this, then chances are you recently found out you or someone you love has cancer. Your world is about to change big-time, and you're looking for some answers and direction. How/what do I know? As I'm writing this, I am just a few days away from finishing up my last cycle of chemo, which concludes a year and five months of cancer treatment. Just before that was the surgery to remove the tumor, then surgery to implant a port in my chest, and then, somewhere in the middle of it all, was CyberKnife surgery to get the cancer cells that had spread to my left lung. I know how you feel. I've been there, done that, and got the gorgeous scars to prove it.

You know, we've just met, and yet I know something about you already. You are loved. If someone gave you this book, it's because that person doesn't want you to worry (and possibly they wanted to be promoted to the top of the list of your ultra cool and brilliant friends by giving you the best book ever). They want you to stick around on this planet, and if you bought this for yourself, then good for you. You are now promoted to the top of my list of ultra cool and brilliant people. You love yourself enough to want to kick this thing's ass, and believe you me that is the best place to start.

There's another thing you should know before you read this. If you've ever read any of my blogs (www.AliGilmoreMusic.com), then you know I'm not a big fan of grammar or spelling rules and regulations. I'm smart. I went to school. I got As in English (when I wanted to) and I understand the value of a grammatical system.

I do. I just prefer to write more like the way I speak, and I don't speak like an English textbook. Faaar from it. So, when I tend to elongate words in speaking, I do so in writing. I also am NOT a fan of the exclamation point. To me, it sounds like yelling. I like to use the tilde (~) instead. It seems more lyrical, and that's how my voice comes across when I'm excited about something (unless I'm yelling or quoting someone else, and then I use the exclamation point). I know the exclamation point is also used to express emphasis. For that, I prefer to capitalize the word. Hrmmm…what else. Oh yeah, I also tend to swear. Sometimes, I swear a lot. When I was younger one of my brothers asked me if I swore because it made me feel all grown-up, which confused me. I don't think I ever wanted to be a "grown-up." I like to swear because it's a satisfying release like a belch or that other thing most women pretend we don't do when we're around others. I wonder if that's how spontaneous combustion started... Ah, right, where was I? Yes…a friend of mine informed me that, "swearing is less offensive if you mistype it." So there you have it. I also like to use the infamous "dot, dot, dot" whenever I pause for effect. I think that's about it. Last, but not least I am still experiencing the joys of "chemo brain" so even with the help of a highly skilled editor you may come across something that doesn't quite fit into a sentence or paragraph or ehm, chapter. Sorry, I know it's annoying. Just take is as an example of what's ahead for you…So, if that stuff doesn't drive you around the bend, then proceed. If it does, then WTH? Hellooooooooo…you've got caaaancer~ Don't you think you've got bigger fish to fry than sticking your nose up at some illiterate smartarse's refusal to follow grammatical rules?

Ok then, here it is…my gift to you. Here's a little heads-up/insider info that should bring some peace of mind. Life offers few guarantees. We are born, we live, and then we go off to the great beyond. If you're not quite ready for the last one, then you'd better buck up now and get ready for the fight of (for) your life. It's also important to note that this book in no way means any disrespect to those who've fought and lost. Not every battle can be won, and every life has its own timeline. No one (and I mean nobody) can promise your outcome, but a big, no, huuuuge part of it is up to you. My hope is this guide will smooth the path you're on and brings a little light to an otherwise darker chapter in this thing called life.

———

Chapter 1:

SO, YOU'VE GOT IT. NOW WHAT?

❖ ❖ ❖

So, the doc broke the bad news to you (gently or not so gently), and your head is reeling. Oh…I so get where you are coming from. I swear. I got my bit of news on my birthday of all days. For some reason, I expected it to be a happy, let's celebrate kind of follow-up appointment, so I made it for an hour before meeting up with friends for the so-called celebration. I think I drank four or five martinis that night. I don't even like martinis, but I love my friends, and we were all looking forward to celebrating, so that's what we did. I laughed at the stories and jokes and smiled like a Cheshire cat. All the while, the words, "Technically, it's stage IV" kept whirling around my brain like a buzz saw. Man oh man, how I wish someone had been there in that moment to do a quiet slide under the table. "Psst…here's a guide that'll get you through it all. No worries. Now go enjoy the party." Then they'd leave me with a comforting wink and a nod.

So, what's next? ASK QUESTIONS. The very first question out of your mouth should be, "Can you fix it?" If you haven't asked already, then ask NOW fer fkssake. Make 'em look you in the eye and tell you straight up what the chances are and what treatment will entail. I asked the day I found out, and Dr. H. looked me straight in the eye and said, "Yes, but it'll be a long road." I responded with, "So, what's the drama about then? If you can fix it, then let's get to it." I think he's still baffled by my wide-eyed optimism, but I swear it (along with excellent medical care) saved my life.

After they tell you your treatment plan, ask for a list of side effects. This is *muy importante*. I'll explain further about that in the "Bigger Boat" chapter. For now, focus on asking questions.

To the Doc:
- Can you fix it? If you don't like the answer, get a second and third opinion.
- How long will treatment take from start to finish? This is very important. I wasn't clear on this answer, and it cost me a lot of time, money, and stress in the end.
- What are the side effects? You'll see why in chapter five.
- How long before the side effects kick in?
- How long do they last after chemo?
- What supplements should I be taking? Ask about vitamin D.
- Why me? Why this particular cancer? They won't have a definitive answer, but you know you want to ask it, so go on.

Find out if your insurance company covers:
- Inpatient (if surgery is part of the treatment plan).
- Outpatient (Port implants are considered outpatient surgery).
- CyberKnife (if it's part of the treatment plan).
- Home med equipment (if you have to use a portable chemo unit).
- Office visits (specialist and regular).

Also ask your insurance company:
- Is the center where you'll get treatment in their network?
- What about fertility treatments? If you're still fertile and want kids, you need to look at your options, like freezing your stuff. Chemo doesn't just kill c cells. It can cause infertility, so be prepared.

What if you don't have insurance? It's harder but not impossible. Contact your state disability office, tell them your situation, and ask what your options are. Of the dozens of people I've spoken to at that office only one was unsympathetic, but he sounded like a miserable git with no love for life or people, so I let him and his crappy outlook roll right off my shoulders. Then I pretended I said in parting, "I may have cancer, but there's a treatment for it, and one day I'll be well, while you, sir, are a soddy tool, and guessing by the entrenched whine in your tone, you will be one for the rest of your underappreciated life." These imaginary moments do come in handy, believe you me.

Make sure you ask all these questions before you start treatment. Once you start, I can tell you, it won't be long before chemo brain sets in, which is this nice, foggy kind of Alzheimer-y thing. You think you're on top of things, but you will lose your train of thought mid-sentence, look at people you know and totally forget their names, or pull up to your house and realize you left the groceries in the cart at the store. Then you realize you never actually made it to the grocer, but you did go to the gas station, and you left your wallet on top of the pump. You think I'm exaggerating for comedic effect? I nearly pulled away from the pump one day while the nozzle was still in my tank. Luckily, the guy in the car behind me honked several times, and the owner came running out and threatened to charge me a thousand dollars if I had driven off and ruined his pump. I was blonde at the time. This is clue number one why I dyed it very, very dark brown. We all have this spaciness to some degree (and most of my friends will tell you it wasn't that much different from who I was before), but chemo enhances it like you wouldn't believe. Blonde or not, you will become a great argument for those jokes. The good part is you'll have your trusty c card. You can flash that, and not a soul will dare poke fun at you. Ha haaaaaa~ You will see that every cloud, even this potentially dark and stormy one, has a silver lining.

I'll talk about it more in the following chapters, but another question between you, yourself, your doc, and your boss (if you're currently working) is, "Should I go on medical leave?" It's no time to be a workaholic, which was my MO, and if your job or workplace is stressful, then the answer is a resounding YES. If that's the case, then you need to check with your company to see if you have supplemental disability insurance. State disability is pretty fair, but it's still only about 60 percent of your salary, and if you're anything like me, that's tough to manage. Because of the decline in the economy, I was already making only about 60 percent of my salary before I'd moved from Seattle back to California. Learning to adjust to another dip in income was a challenge for sure, and believe me, any stress is a bad thing for you right now. So ask yourself if continuing to work is going to help you on this road or hurt you. Only you really know the answer to that.

———

Chapter 2:

THE UPSIDE
(OR EVERY CLOUD HAS ITS SILVER LINING)

I had finished the first draft of this book and sent it off to someone for review when I woke up thinking about it and what my friend, Jen, had posted on Facebook. Here's a copy and paste of it:

Jen Lilly
January 12 ✲

Life is too short for constant complaining and negativity. I'm turning over a new leaf. We have so many things to be thankful for every day that we are lucky enough to wake up. Gratitude, people . . . hop on the train!

Unlike · Comment · Share   👍 46 💬 16

This came shortly after her breaking the sad news that her nephew Rhys Harrod (that's his little face there) had suddenly passed away, showing us again just how unpredictable life can be... I met Rhys' mom, Cat recently and didn't feel it was right to broach the subject then, but as I got to know her was picturing him in the great beyond going on about how awesome his life was here. It was easy to envision given the people that surrounded him.

Jen and I met through work a few years back, and I knew from my first interview she and I would end up good friends. We have a similar outlook on life. We tend to take on others' burdens, but we also have a great (ENORMOUS) capacity for love. When we take on too much "crap," it bogs us down, and we get, well, bitchy. She had every reason to be bitchy (I can spell this one out because it's not technically "a swear") when she posted this, but some kind of switch flipped in her that day, and she saw the silver lining. You have those friends, right? They are great at helping you put things back into perspective and allowing you to do the same for them when they need it.

It's like when I had the gall to go on and ooooon (for months) about how upset I was with all the weight I was gaining during chemo. It averaged four pounds every other week for a year and a half. Yup…that's a lot by anyone's standards. She was getting increasingly irritated with me, though. At one point, I thought she was going to flip the café table over on me, and it didn't even occur to me until the next day what it was she wanted to say. She was trying to contain it and give me my bitchy moment.

Jen lost her mom (Victoria Ann Swankie) to cancer just a few short years back and after a long and vicious battle. It was shortly after I'd started working at the same company as her. We've had many conversations about how the loss of our moms (mine was a cancer survivor who died, for lack of a better term, of old age) affects our lives to this day. We also discovered our moms had a lot in common, and we like to imagine they're up in the ethereal "there" and having nice chats about us over tea. We lament about how much we took them for granted when we were younger and still unaffected by death, which was like a distant relative you knew existed but had never met face-to-face. She'd said the words before, but I think she knew I wasn't capable of hearing them that day. She wanted to remind me how lucky I was to even be alive and, instead of worrying about some extra weight or puffiness, I should remind myself how temporary that is. I should enjoy what I could such as not having to sit at a desk that moment trying to meet the demands of the working world. Instead, I was sitting in a cool café, eating delicious food (I do so love that), and spending time with a good friend.

Hey, we all have our freak-out moments, and we're allowed them. Don't forget, though, to shift to the lighter side of it when you're done. Yes, you have it bad. You may even have the worst case of cancer since the inception of cancer. Maybe they're thinking of renaming your type of cancer after you because it's so rare, mystifying, and devastating. OK. Just remember that no matter how bad you've got it, someone else out there has it worse. A girl got her arm bit clean off by a shark. Do you want to trade places with that one? Hrmmmm? How about Superman? He was out happy-go-luckily riding his horse one day, fell off, and spent the rest of his days in a wheelchair and numb from the neck down. May I add that neither one went around moping. Nope, they persevered and got on with their lives. It's OK to feel what you feel. Just don't let it suck you into that long, dark tunnel that cuts you off from the rest of the world or the amazing-ness it offers up on a silver platter nearly every day.

Awesome. What the hell does all that have to do with the title of this chapter? I know, I tend to digress (or stray or whatever you like to call it) from the main point. My friend PB calls it "stream of consciousness" writing. I write how I think, as I'm thinking it, which makes the job of the poor, dear, well-educated editor of this book not an easy one, I'm sure. Dear editor of this book: sorry I'm such a pain in the ass and that you got stuck with this assignment. I owe you a pint or a box of chocolates or something~

A few days later, Jen posted a pic of herself surfing for the first time, and a flurry of positive responses followed. I'm not saying you should hop and skip your way through your cancer experience as if nothing bothers you. Do, however, take a look at some of the brighter moments available. For myself, it was the first time in my working life where I wasn't tied to a daily routine. I am by nature (like my dear ole dad) a workaholic and a creature of rituals. I have always loved the challenge of starting out in a job and excelling quickly. I love to "fix" broken things and "improve" lacking things. I thrive on it. Unfortunately, I get too caught up in it and forget to savor life outside of work, which brings us to the upside. With the c -card, you are given the opportunity to set pretty much everything and everyone else aside and focus primarily on you. Some people love work, and good for them. They can continue if it helps them, but most of us are working to pay the bills. Pose this question to yourself: If you won the lottery today, would you continue working where you work? Now you have your answer.

Also, if you're the kind who just quietly takes it when people are cold or rude to you, you'll love flashing the c card in front of them. I remember going to the post office to get my passport renewed. It had expired, and I wanted to make sure it was handy when all this chemo stuff was over, and I could hopefully travel to an exotic holiday getaway such as Ireland, Italy, or even Isla Mujeres. The woman in charge of passport renewals was a sour little snit who really didn't have time for my dimwit (chemo) brain. This is clue number two as to why I dyed my hair very, very dark brown. She made this clear with every sigh and snide remark until I said, "Sorry, I know this must be annoying for you. Chemo brain...sucks. I'm renewing my passport in hopes to go to Mexico after the cancer treatment is over. Only a few more months to go." Then I gave a weak but effortful smile. By the time I walked out of there, I was practically family. I don't suggest you do that to every snot box out there. Just do it when you feel the push to. The truth is she wasn't a bad person. She was just caught in that tunnel. Another silver lining is that your c card can help others snap out of it and look on the brighter side of things. Not bad, eh? Yes, it sucks for you that you work in a post office and have to wear that unflattering uniform…but would you rather have cancer like that lady? Hrmmm?

———

Chapter 3:

SHOW NO FEAR

❖ ❖ ❖

I've said it before and I'll say it again, cancer is nothing more than a bully. No, seriously. It goes around kicking the crap out of your healthy cells until they give in and join its gang or die trying to defend themselves. I strongly believe it feeds on fear, anxiety, and repression. Haven't you heard that saying, "He's going to stress himself into an early grave" or "She was worried sick"?

So, how do you beat a bully? You can pretend to ignore it or at least refuse to give it credence for starters. I do this by refusing to capitalize its name. Why, the main reason there's a second edition of this book is because cancer was the first word in this chapter, so the editor capitalized it (as they should the first word) and I just couldn't stand it. That may be silly, but the mind is a very powerful thing, and every time I use a lowercase letter, I imagine it shrinking in strength. Anytime I hear it mentioned on TV or radio, I flip it the bird. When in public, I do so under the table. For decades now, we've cowered at the mention of it and understandably so, but modern medicine has been catching up to cancer, and so should our perception of it. Again, I'm not trying to give anyone false hope. I just think we should move beyond the darker images and gut-wrenching emotions from the days of *Terms of Endearment* and face this little fecker with determination. Maybe then we can relegate it to the ranks of other diseases that are mere shadows in history.

So, the first step in fighting back is showing NO FEAR. When people around you are afraid for you, reassure them you're not afraid, and they shouldn't be either. I know, I know. You ARE afraid.

Trust me when I tell you that you must STOP THAT immediately. Seriously just STOP IT. Oh, this brings something to mind as I'm writing this. Do you remember the comedian Bob Newhart? He did this hilarious skit on some show I can't remember the name of, but it was funny and oh so apropos. Go ahead. Google it or go to YouTube and search for it now: Bob Newhart Stop It. Go watch it, and then, when you're done laughing, come back. It's cool…I'll wait here.

So? Is he funny or what? Did it make you forget for a second the huge burden you've been lugging around? Good. Every time you start to feel weighed down by all of this, I want you to remember Bob's voice saying, "STOP IT." Do whatever it takes to find your happy place and/or fake it till you make it, baby. Your life depends on it. The more positive energy you emit, the greater the chances of survival. Hey, If you want me to go darker I will. So what if you don't make it? What if you only have six months left in this life as you know it? Do you really want to spend it buried under a pile of stress and regrets, or would you rather spend it laughing, loving, and enjoying life? I'll give you two guesses what my choice was/is.

I was sitting around the table with a few friends recently when one friend asked me what was at the top of my to-do list now that it was all done. I made a grandiose statement about love, but later in the evening, as I soaked in who I was with and how we all were around each other, I said, "Y'know what? This…this is what I want most and more of." As I sat around the table with another group of friends the other night, I smiled and was thoroughly pleased with myself for reaching out and getting more of what I really wanted out of life.

This brings to mind a moment with a good friend's husband. He's known for not mincing his words. Sometimes this is thigh-slapping hilarious, and sometimes it's inappropriate with a capital "I," but he usually gets by the easily offended brigade with his charming Galway accent. Anyway, when I was first diagnosed and word was out, a lot of friends would look at me with that pained expression as if they were trying not to cry. I did look somewhat like a train wreck, I admit. We were gathered around at our favorite sushi joint one night (I watched, and they ate), and he happened to be sitting next to me. We were talking about something that touched on the subject, and he gave me a wry smile, shrugged his shoulders, and said, "Ah well. We all gotta go sometime." I can't tell you how good it felt to hear him say that. We hugged in that moment. It was probably the most honest hug we've ever shared, and I reminded him of that moment recently over sushi (it's one of our favorite group outings can't you tell).

It's funny how, in that moment, we take things to heart, but the very next day, we can just as easily fall back into our somewhat deluded perception that life goes on, and it's business as usual. Even with all I've experienced this past year and half, I still have moments where I get caught up in the dramas of day-to-day life, and little annoyances drive my temper to a boil. Human nature is such a wild and beguiling mystery at times. Will that particular piece of the puzzle be solved once we reach the other side? I am curious... but am in noooo rush to find out.

So, we touched on it, but we have to go there if we're really going to show NO fear. If this is news to you, then I'm sorry to be the one to break it to you, but, ehm, you ARE going to die. Well, you are going to die one day, that is. Unless you are immortal, and it's yet to be proven that anyone is, then we all are going to croak/kick the bucket at some point. If you haven't accepted it yet, then get over it already, and stop watching stupid movies such as *Final Destination XXI* that portray death as some vindictive bastard that will chase you down and make you pay in the worst way if you dare cheat it. Death isn't sporting for a brawl, or some psycho killer on the loose randomly striking people down because it's in a bad mood. Also, fer fkssake, you did NOT get cancer because you bullied that other kid in grade school and never made amends. Death is not a punishment but a means to an end. It is cause and effect, if you will. You are born, so, therefore, at some point you'll die.

Besides, when you think on it, no one really dies as long as there is something or someone to remember them by, right?

As for the "Why me?" does it really matter how you got cancer? You can dig and research from here to Timbuktu and back, but it's not going to change the fact you have cancer. I say leave it to the experts to discover causes and cures, and let me spend my energy on situations I can change. It's there, and it's not going away on its own, so think of this as a gentle reminder that you are going to die at some point. If your life got off track from what you wanted it to be, take this momentous opportunity to get it back on track.

While you're at it, if you haven't already, you might as well buck up and get that last W&T put together. You may not have a pot to piss in, but believe it or not, there are things of yours that loved ones will consider of great value and they'll want to have them to remember you by.

A great example is my mom's rolling pin. It wasn't valuable per se, but I was very fond of it. It reminded me of better times with her (we bickered a lot), and I wanted it after she was gone. My mom didn't have a will that detailed who got what, which can be a bad thing. I am lucky, however, in that my dad, brothers, and sister all knew how to play fair. We gathered around one day long after (probably too long after) my mom had passed, spread out everything, and asked each other who wanted what. We went through her teapots, stemware, sewing and craft stuff, and more. I was surprised at what was important to others but not at all surprised at how well we worked together to sort it all out. That doesn't always happen, though, so save those you leave behind the hassle, and put together a will. Update it every now and then when your list of valuables changes. This also helps keep you grounded in the reality that you are not immortal and should live every day to the fullest.

Another element to the whole embracing life thing is to stop doing the stupid things that just beg for serious health troubles. We all have our vices, and we all know which ones are really hurting us, so you'll get no pointing of fingers or lecturing here. I'll just out myself on this one, all right?

Now, anyone who knows me considers me a Pollyanna of sorts (well, most everyone does; I can be a real brat sometimes), but what many (and I'm still surprised by this) didn't know is that I have always been anxious. It was big smiles on the outside but shaking like a Chihuahua on the inside. My mind would hyper-analyze whatever I was about to deal with till my heart felt it would nearly burst out of my chest, and then I'd light up a cig and breathe in…breathe out…and calm myself. That's how I dealt with it for nearly twenty years. I'd light up a cig every time I felt it creeping on, which added up to anywhere between a pack to two packs a day. OK, yes, I also used them to manage my weight because, if you didn't catch it before, I love to eat…just looove it.

When it was clear I was in some kind of serious health trouble, I asked my doc for a prescription to help curb my anxiety (the trigger) so I could kick the twenty-something-year habit. It seemed ludicrous (even to my thick head) to expect the doctors to fix me when I was doing plenty of damage on my own. Like a baaaad but horribly attractive ex, I miss cigarettes to this day. Yet I got there had to be some compromise on my part. More than that, though, I had to take part in the healing. I couldn't leave all the work up to the doctors and nurses if I really expected to take any credit for my recovery, and so that was it. That was in April, and by September I had undergone the surgery to remove the tumor in my colon (charmingly referred to as a Sigmoidectomy). I was happy to see how much faster I recovered from it than if I'd still been a smoker.

OK, I know I said I wouldn't point any fingers, but I'm an ex-smoker, which makes me a sanctimonious liar (at times). This still bothers me to this day, so I'll tell the story.

I was sitting there at the cancer center getting pumped full of chemo one day. I had my headphones on, but this still doesn't drown out others talking away. So I heard this older woman telling her friend how she still smokes. She said she enjoys it, and she's not quitting no matter what they say. I did my best not to shoot daggers, and I kept on with Facebook or e-mail or whatever I was doing on my laptop. The imaginary conversation went like this, however: I took my headphones off, leaned in toward her, and said, "Ohhh, I think it's marvelously defiant of you to refuse to quit something that's significantly causing you harm and decreasing your chances of ever recovering from cancer. Good for you for sticking to your principles. Now, how 'bout you go FCK OFF, and stop wasting everyone's time and energy?" At this point, I put my headphones back on, leaned back, and continued whatever it was I was doing on my laptop.

Hey, even if you're not prone to anxiety or depression, you may want to consider going on something during the duration of your treatment. I highly recommend it (no pun intended). I went with Welbutron (Bupropion) because, from what I'd read, it seemed the simplest. It was like the aspirin of antidepressants. I'm not keen on the fancier new meds with all their bells and whistles. I had to skip the night dosage (it kept me wiiiide awake), but other than that, I felt no side effects. It was just a nice little wave of calm that washed over me whenever the anxiety tried to well up.

Don't dig taking a pill? Then check with a naturopath or the cool lady at the health-food store for a natural supplement. Every body and mind is different, so find whatever works best for you, but be sure to consult with your oncology doc before spending any money on remedies. Whatever you do, don't be naive in thinking you've got all the raw, positive energy needed to deal with this. Pollyanna may be my middle name, and though I took my happy pills religiously, I still had my dark moments. Once I knew I was in the clear, I weaned myself off them, and other than a few "moments" (that most people experience), I've been fine and pretty much anxiety-free. Oh look, it's another silver lining~ So let's say it: SHOW NO FEAR~ Go ahead...say it loud and proud. I even used this saying the other day when my tour guide pushed my sea kayak out into the water and toward the scary waves (whopping two-footers). I said it under my breath so as not to appear too dorky, but I said it with true conviction. It feels really good I'm telling you~

So, here's where I hope you are now. You know what your treatment plan is, and you have an added boost (herbal or RX) to help you keep in calm waters through it all. You are FEARLESS and ready to take on the next addition to your arsenal.

———

Chapter 4:

YOU AND YOUR PORT

❖ ❖ ❖

No, I'm not talking about the kind of port that comes in bottles or the one ships sail into, though those are both lovely. This will be the shortest chapter because there's not much to say on the subject. You need one. You'll get one. You'll eventually forget you have it, and then one day they'll remove it. It may all seem weird at first, but trust me, before you know it, you'll be so glad you have one. I didn't have much time to get used to the idea of having one. I think I underwent the procedure about a week after they told me I needed one, and then just a few days after that, I started chemo.

A port is this little thing they implant just under the skin in your chest (sometimes arm or abdomen) that has a tube running from it to a major vein. It's where they draw your blood for weekly labs, and it is the entry port for the chemo to get into your system. It may seem icky, but it beats getting poked in the arm or hand every week. That's not possible anyway because some of us have to take the little chemo unit home with us.

How do I describe a port? It's like one of those rubber balls that glows in the dark and bounces off the walls, but it's cut in half and hollowed out. A tube is attached to one end, and the other end is attached to the jugular vein in your neck. Creating a little pocket inside the skin of your chest for it to sit in, it's all just under the skin. You can barely see mine. People always hesitate when I offer to let them touch it, but they say it's kind of cool.

Mostly the scar on the neck shows, but that's only visible if you're standing pretty close. I asked Dr. C. (who installed mine) how long I would have it in my body, and he shrugged his unworried shoulders and said he had some patients who have had theirs for over ten years. I don't know if that's necessary since most places that draw blood won't use it. They have to use a special hook like needle to access it (no, it doesn't hurt), and they're a lot more expensive than the regular kind. So, at some point after you're done with your treatment and in the clear, you should have it removed. I wanted to have mine removed before this book was published, thus reinforcing the validity of the statement, "I beat cancer" as opposed to, "I'm beating cancer." Dr. H. convinced me, however, that waiting a year wasn't such a bad idea. If nothing else, it would be nice to give my body a break from anything medically invasive.

Back to the beginning, though. I'm not sure if it helps to hear all this beforehand or if it's better to just go in blind, but I think it would've helped me to understand what was happening well in advance instead of moments before the procedure. Again, I was on happy pills, so who knows? This is considered an outpatient procedure, so you'll check into the hospital outpatient surgery, and a nice nurse will keep your mind occupied with chitchat while prepping you for it. The nurse will show you what a port looks like and mentally walk you through how it's implanted and how it'll work for you. It looks like a harmless toy. The nurse will also show you the type of needle used to access it during your treatment, which looks like a mini harpoon. The odd thing about the procedure is you'll be awake. Don't worry. You are fully, and I mean fully, anesthetized, and you have a big, blue sheet above your face so you don't see any of the gruesomeness, but it was a bit freaky/odd to be talking away with Dr. C. and the nurses while I couldn't see them. For some reason, I could feel blood dripping down my neck, but there was no pain, I swear. Even after it all, I didn't feel any pain in the incision areas. You have to have someone to take you home from the hospital, though. They won't let you take a cab. I tried. This is one of those moments where you let people who love you do their part. Trust me, they want to, so fer fkssake, let them help already.

———

Chapter 5:

LAY YOUR CARDS ON THE TABLE

❧ ❧ ❧

I was pretty protective of my privacy during the whole ordeal, but there was one thing I did in the very beginning when rumors were flying, and people didn't know what (if anything) to say. I don't know if this was the best way to do it, but it was my way.

I started off by sending a group e-mail to most of my local friends. These were the ones who'd see me face-to-face while this was all happening. It was an up-front, no-holds-barred e-mail. It was the first time I wrote out the words "stage IV," and it shook me up a bit, but I knew I had to tell them all the same story. It had to be the true story all at once if I was to get any peace. They were, after all, already assuming the worst. Plus, I wanted to be sure it stayed off my personal Facebook page. I wanted to keep that place lighthearted with all the bantering and social escapes it offered. "Hey, everybody. I've got cancer, and it's stage IV~" just didn't seem the kind of status update Facebook was designed for. In the email I told them my prognosis, the plan, and what I needed from them. First and foremost, I needed them not to worry. I went on to explain that when they worried, I stressed out because I didn't want them to worry which meant their worrying and stress impeded my healing process, so it would actually be detrimental to me if they worried.

I also asked them not to treat me like I was sick. "If you treat me like I'm sick, I'll act like I'm sick," I said. This is the case with treating bullies. If you play sick so you can stay home from school or work and avoid the bully, that bully knows and feeds off it. "Ha ha…you're too scared of me to show up." So, go on with your life and enjoy many of the same things and some new ones while you're at it. Just do it in smaller doses. This way you reserve the majority of your energy for the treatments and recovery. I laughed and flirted with my docs and befriended my nurses, which was really easy, by the way. They were all so very cool. Smiling, laughing, flirting, and joking…these all increase the endorphins in your body, and we all know endorphins are a good thing. I envisioned them as little rays of sunbeams blasting light onto the dark matter (another word I use for cancer cells) lurking about in my body.

The last thing I said was that I wanted them to feel free to talk about it openly to me or amongst themselves. I wasn't trying to keep this a deep, dark secret. I wanted it to become matter-of-fact. When you tell people you've got cancer, they tend to want to give you the shirt off their back. It's not necessary. It made me uncomfortable, and I sort of felt like they'd be disappointed if I got well after all the fuss they'd gone to. Then again, maybe it was just me on that one. Oh, I couldn't resist. I did make a point to my smoking friends that I wasn't going to judge or harp on them, but they should probably pay close attention to the details of the crap I was going through. They'd probably be needing that info for future reference. What, I already admitted I can be kind of a brat sometimes.

I'm already living to regret this part, so heed my warning. There were some people back home who I never told. I didn't exclude anyone out of malice or lack of regard. Oddly enough, the ones I didn't tell were because I thought they would worry the most, and I couldn't stand the thought of it. I even lied to my dad and said it was just a tumor. This is a baaad idea, peeps. Eventually someone (like maybe your sister) is going to slip up and it'll make those people worry all the more. After all, if you lied about that, what else are you not telling them? It's a lot of pressure asking someone to keep a secret like that. It's also kind of unfair, don't you think? Do you see how best intentions are good to scrutinize after putting them in motion? I need a full-time person for that, let me tell you.

OK, so you've got all your questions answered, you are now fearless, and all your loved ones are in the know and clear on what you need. What's next?

————

Chapter 6:

THINK SPRING CUZ IT'S TIME TO CLEAN

❄ ❄ ❄

FYI, several cities have these amazing groups that offer services such as free housecleaning to those going through cancer treatment. I've never been keen about having strangers go through all my dirt, but if you're not a wing nut like me on that front, then by all means, whip out that c card, and come home to a nice, clean place to plop your tired self down after your sessions. If you're a do-it-yourselfer like me, here's another thing to do before you start your treatment. Go through those piles of papers busting out of your desk space and kitchen drawers, clean out that goop living in your fridge, wipe the layers of dust off the fan blades and lamps, stock up on antibacterial wipes, soap dispensers, and cleaning gloves, and for crying out loud, get rid of all those clothes you are never, eeeever going to wear. Replace them with super comfy stuff. I bought one of those ultrasoft "Life is good" sweatshirts. When I'm feeling extra crappy, I love to put that thing on along with my super fuzzy slippers and just curl up with a good flat screen.

There's another kind of spring cleaning that needs doing. I'm sure you know where we're headed with this one. It's time to take note of those you hang out with that make you feel energized and those that suck the life out of you. No, this is not a legitimate excuse to pack up your kids or spouse and drop them off at the nearest adoption agency. It's also important to cut back on the cocktails. I am a huge fan of happy hour and nights out with friends that turn into, "Is it morning already? Let's make a big breakfast!"

But your body can't take it like before. How dare I say this when I just said, "enjoy life as you like it," right? I still mean enjoy life; just do it in smaller doses. Alcohol is lovely, but it *de*hydrates big-time, and your body needs to HYDRATE like you've never hydrated before. It also needs rest like you're a ninety-year-old professional napper. A veritable Grandpa Simpson you'll be…yup.

To give you an example of what I mean on the peeps side of it, one patient told me about a friend of hers who kept saying, "WE have cancer." "Yeah…no," I'd say. "I have cancer. You just have a screw loose." You know who these people are. Sometimes you hang out with them because you feel for them, or you feel normal next to them. You can still love them. Just do it at arm's length for now. I can't emphasize enough how important it is to keep a tight hold on your energy reserve. Once you're well again, you can always go back to your old ways, but by then you might be seeing just a wee bit clearer the correlation between the way you handled stressors in your past and the state of your health today. I'm just saying…

I am writing this from the perspective of someone who lives solo, but if you share a home with others, I hope you can carve out a space where you can just be on your own when you need to. Sometimes we just need to not talk at all, soak in a marathon of our favorite show, or find mental escape in a good book. Not having live-ins to help out was taxing a bit at times, but having peace and quiet whenever I wanted was a nice compromise.

So, let's see…you've got all your questions answered, you are now fearless, all your loved ones are in the know and clear on what you need, and your house and head are clean as a whistle. Now it's time to get a bigger boat.

———

Chapter 7:

WE'RE GOING TO NEED A BIGGER BOAT (EH, MEDICINE CABINET)

❧ ❧ ❧

That's right. If you haven't already, head into your bathroom with a garbage bag, and throw out all the crap in the medicine cabinet (diet pills, outdated prescriptions, and anything else you don't use). I'd be surprised if you'll even be able to close the cabinet door once you're done filling it with your new arsenal of feel-good items. I made a new friend at chemo on my last cycle. It was her first day, and I surprised myself how I couldn't stop talking about all the things I wish I'd known on my first day. I promised to make her a list of medicine cabinet items she'd need. I think that's when the seed was planted to write this whole thing. It was cemented when one of my good friends back home told me her mom was just diagnosed, and she asked for advice. I was so frustrated to see her so worried, and I wished I'd written this long before so I could've just handed it to her and her mom and put them immediately at ease.

Side effects…this is a tough one to cover because there are so many, and they vary depending on what type of cancer you have. Believe it or not, there are many different types of cancer and different types of drug treatments, which have different side effects. A common misconception (that I had up until the day of my orientation) was that all cancer patients lose their hair. This is not true it turns out. That is a side effect of the drug that treats cancers in reproductive areas and possibly others, but I'm no expert on that. If they tell you you're going to lose your hair, you're either going to shrug because you don't mind or you're already bald or, if it were me, I'd say *cool*. That would mean I would get to try a bunch of different hair colors and styles I wouldn't normally. Plus, I love wearing hats anyway, so it would be no big whoop.

I did not get the chance to say that since going bald was not a side effect I experienced. Instead (probably because I was already hypothyroid), I gained well (and I mean weeeeell) over fifty pounds in the year and a half of treatment. I complained at every sitting with Dr. H., but he just gave me a blank stare. Sometimes a sigh of exhaustion slid under it, and he reminded me that weight gain was not a matter of concern right now. Each time he'd say this with increasing emphasis until he finally belted out that he had some patients who were so thin he could actually see their organs bulging through their concave bellies (i.e., Ali...I've got bigger fish to fry than your vanity's struggle over weight gain). I tried my best to avoid that subject from then on, but I continued to whine to anyone else that would listen. Every time I'd mention it to my friend, Jen, who was studying to be a nurse, she'd remind me it was a good thing. It would help my body fight the good fight. I don't even care if that's true. I loved her for saying it because it DID make me feel better about it. It's ironic, don't you think? There I was, skating along the edge of life or death, and I couldn't stop lamenting over weight gain. Ohhh, the mighty mind versus the whimpering ego.

Another side effect you can't treat with meds is sensitivity to light and sun. This is where you'll break out in bumps and sometimes blisters from what you'd consider normal exposure to the sun. If this is one of your side effects, just wear sun protective clothing and at least SPF 50 on any exposed skin. Keep that sun exposure to small, small doses. I can tell you that I did NOT listen to that advice, and during one of my breaks, I thought I would be fine in the sun. It had been at least a couple weeks since my last chemo session so, no problem right? We had another one of our friends' day outings. About sixteen of us hopped on our beach cruisers and did a house crawl. We stopped at each of our houses (there were seven within a three-mile radius), and at each one was a different food/drink served. I made homemade blueberry and cranberry muffins and mimosas with grapefruit, cranberry, and lemon. What, I was on a break. So it went until sundown when we met up at the last house, grilled, and sat around a bonfire. See... this is what I mean by enjoying life. Though my lovely and protective friends all took turns spraying me head-to-toe throughout the day, we did miss a spot...the lips. Even with my baseball cap on all day, they managed to get burnt. They were crispy, blistery, thoroughly painful, and embarrassingly burnt, which lasted well over a week. So, please, for the love of Pete, take heed. These are pearls I'm giving you. Pearls I tell you~

Another side effect is sensitivity to cold. This one I shrugged at when they told me. Even as I started chemo, I thought it was minor at worst. I was not thinking it was cumulative, as in the more chemo you get, the stronger the side effect becomes. A couple of months into it, I had to wear gloves at night if there was any hint of chill. The cool air bit like it was winter in the frozen tundra. That wasn't the worst of it, though. Any surface such as a car door handle, fridge, or microwave was biting to the touch. The trick was to wear long-sleeve shirts and pull the bottom of the sleeve over your hand before touching anything like that. I don't care if it's August, and blazing heat is running through your home...don't even think about trying to eat or drink anything from the fridge or even something so-called "room temperature." It's like swallowing an ice cube. No...that's putting it mildly. I don't know...dry ice? I've never swallowed dry ice before, but I imagine it would better describe this side effect.

One other side effect worth mentioning more than once is that cotton mouth/chemical thing that lines your mouth and sinuses. I'm pretty sure everyone gets to experience this lovely one. You can rinse to get rid of the cotton, but the chemical ick taste will stick, and anything milder than Vindaloo or five alarm chili will taste just plain ole weird. I've said it a couple times in this book, but I'll say it again here...avoid all the foods and beverages you love. If you don't, they will forever be ruined by the chemical ick. Stick to spicy and citrus flavors, and you'll be fine.

Let's go back to the cabinet. As I said, I made a list. Now, these are the side effects I dealt with. There are other ones out there, but these I can tell you about first hand. Keep this list handy. You'll be glad to have it there at the ready when your symptoms kick in. Before you go out and buy any of these remedies, be sure to go over the list with your doc, and make sure they agree. They're the boss of you. I'm not~

Side Effect and Relievers

1. Nausea—Ativan (and Mary Jane)
2. The runs—Imodium A-D
3. To soothe the burning ring of fire—Tucks medicated wipes or Preparation H
4. The log jam—MiraLAX (best taken in small doses every day, see recipe below)
5. Can't sleep—Tylenol PM and Benadryl
6. Can't stop sniffling—Claritin or NyQuil to sleep through it
7. Flu-like symptoms after getting Neupogen or Neulasta shots—Claritin. Take the night before and for four days following the shot.
8. Bloody nose and dry sinuses—saline spray every day
9. Bleeding gums—softer toothbrush and gentle paste. They will still bleed but not as much.
10. Acid reflux—Zantac or the generic version, Ranitidine.
11. Urinary tract infection (UTI) —Drink the cranberry cocktail (see below) at least once a day to keep UTIs at bay and to HYDRATE.
12. Sensitivity to sunlight—Always wear sun protection when outside, and avoid the sun whenever you can until at least four weeks after treatment.
13. Gas—Gas-X. You're going to be drawn to spicy foods, so trust me. I tried the generic brand. It's not even close to as effective, so go for the original. You could also try Beano before you eat.

14. Mouth sores/thrush—Biotene. The moment you feel it come on, swish this around your mouth.
15. Joint aches (as in, it hurts to stand up and walk) —Velvet Antler. I was hard hit by joint aches for months before a friend suggested velvet antler. I tried a couple different brands after, but the purer the better I say. It worked within a couple of short weeks. The pain before was so bad that I kissed the empty bottle before tossing it out.
16. Hot flashes—GNC's Phyto-Estrogen Formula.

You'll also want a thermometer on hand, if you don't already. Having a temperature is a sign of infection, and infections are a very bad thing. You can have one and not even know it, so be sure to take your temp on a regular basis when you're not being seen by the pros. Ask them. They'll tell you how often to check.

The new cranberry cocktail:
1 32-oz bottle of water (suck out ½ cup of it)
Add ¼ cup or more of just cranberry juice (bitter/unsweetened), or add fresh-squeezed lemon or lime to it.
Add ½ cap of MiraLAX, and shake it up good.
Drink one of these in the morning and one in the afternoon/evening as needed.

I asked the nurses if they had any additional suggestions, and Anita mentioned taking thin slices of gingerroot and either sucking on them or putting them in water and drinking that to ease nausea. It makes sense. I'm not a fan of fresh ginger, though. It tastes like soap to me. The thought of it actually makes me a little nauseous, so I'll be skipping out on that one, but it is a great suggestion. I'm thinking back now to how my mom gave us saltine crackers and ginger ale to soothe our tummies, and I remember liking ginger ale, especially the one she grew up with (Vernors) back in Michigan. It's funny how that all ties in together.

Did I already say stay away from the foods/beverages you love? Yes, I did. Just checking to see you were paying attention. On that note, though, there are two kinds of food you need to avoid, regardless of your taste buds. These are grapefruit and raw seafood. Avoid grapefruit because (don't bother asking why) it can interfere with the effectiveness of medication. Avoid raw seafood (of any kind) because of the bacteria it contains. Your body normally can easily deal with that bacteria, but it's too busy fighting off the other stuff during chemo, so you could get incredibly sick. This is no joke. Stay clear from both. I am a sushi lover. Two years living in Tokyo made me a fan for life, and I was used to eating sushi at least once or twice a week. I'm also what you might call a grapefruit addict. I could eat/drink the stuff daily. When I was a smoker, I probably drank sixteen ounces of grapefruit juice every day. Someone once pointed out the craving was probably for the vitamin C because nicotine depletes your body of it. Ohhhh, you will discover many correlations like this as you learn to listen to your body more. That said, putting aside your favorite foods and beverages can be hard, but man oh man, it tastes so good when you finally get back to them~

Right then…you've got all your questions answered, you are obstinately fearless, all your loved ones are in the know, clear on and giving you what you need, your house and head are clean as a whistle, and your medicine cabinet is filled to the brim. It's time to meet up with Mary Jane.

———

Chapter 8:

MAKE FRIENDS WITH MARY JANE

❖ ❖ ❖

There's been some controversy over this subject, but for the most part (at least in California), we've all gotten over it and realized that, though some knuckleheads overuse it to escape, it does have its purposes. I'm one of those that believe in *live and let live*, but if it's illegal, I'm going to stay clear of it. You can take the girl out of the Catholic church, but…

Well, here's another silver lining in your c world. It's now legal for you, and most docs even encourage you to make friends with Mary Jane, aka 420 or marijuana, to help keep nausea at bay and thus maintain your weight. My doctor didn't feel the need to recommend this, however, thanks to my family's policy: eat when you're happy, eat when you're sad, eat when you're sick, and eat even when you're mad. You get the RX from your oncology doc, and then you go to this store that offers a plethora of choices. You can smoke it in a pipe, roll it like a cig, or enjoy it in a Rice Krispy treat. You name it. It's all at your disposal, and you should feel free to indulge. A lot of people also use it to treat their anxiety and swear it works wonders.

Won't getting this RX put me on some kind of government watch or put me at risk for being declined for certain future jobs? Really? Seriously? No. The government approved its use for chemo patients, and any company that wouldn't hire you because you used pot to help curb nausea while being treated for cancer… well, is that the kind of company you'd even want to work for? Say it with me, "HellNoinaHandbasket."

It took me a while to relax on this subject. So I get it if you're unsure. One thing about this unfamiliar road you're walking is that you're going to see, feel, and experience things you may have never thought about. You are going to see life from a whole different perspective. I was going to say your vision would go from myopic to something that sounded broad, but that doesn't quite cut it. It's more like it shatters your image of life into nearly unrecognizable pieces and scatters it all around you. Like…oh, what was that movie with the line, "There is no spoon"? *The Matrix*. It's also like someone handing you a snow globe, and you peer inside to see the life you had before you were handed the c card. It's a beautiful thing. I love that I'm no longer afraid of dying. I'm glad I got an extension on my lease, but I get that life is constantly moving and changing all around us, and I enjoy and experience it far more in-depth now than I did before. I hope the same for you.

So…you've got all your questions answered, you are oh so fearless, all your loved ones are in the know and clear on giving you what you need, your house and head are clean as a whistle, your medicine cabinet is filled to the brim, and you've made a new, super laid-back friend. Now it's time to acquire a new phobia.

———

Chapter 9:

GERMAPHOBES "R" Us

❖ ❖ ❖

All that talk about how you need to chill out and relax, and now I say, what? OK, I don't mean you need to go to the extreme like Howie Mandel who (poor guy) thinks of his palm as a petri dish. Leave OCD to the professionals. You need, however, to become acutely aware of the germs around you and how to stay clear of them whenever possible. When you were younger, did your mother ever say, "put that down" or "take that thing out of your mouth. You don't know where it's been!" It's kind of like that.

One day at chemo, I was noting the names of photos (photography is another passion of mine) that I wanted to come back to later and edit. In between writing, I'd be viewing the images, so I'd put my pen in my mouth until I was ready to use it again. One of the nurses nearly shouted at me from across the room, "Ali, nooooooo! Get that out of your mouth!" You'd think I was about to pull a pin out of a grenade the way she came at me. FYI, I read this to Rachel, and she considers this an over dramatization, but she agrees with the strength of my recommendation to keep items and your hands out of your mouth. Let me add, you should definitely keep these things out of your eyes as well. Conjunctivitis (pink eye) sucks anytime, but it's ten times worse when you're slow to heal. While you're on chemo, my friend, you are definitely slow to heal. I also wear contacts and refuse to invest in a pair of prescription glasses because I'm stupidly vain sometimes. I kept putting my fingers in my eyes, germy fingers…under protected windows to the soul/body, need I say more?

Another way to protect yourself is to send an update to your friends once chemo starts letting them in on your new food and beverage needs. People will want to cook for you, and you should let them, trust me. Gently inform them of your new germ warfare as well. Believe me, many don't make the connection that they need to stay clear if they have anything contagious. This is true even of something seemingly nonthreatening such as the common cold. You need to stock up on antibacterial soaps and wash your hands with it throughout the day. My big mistake was not washing my hands after petting my friend's dogs. I'm allergic, but they're a hypoallergenic breed, so I didn't think twice about it, but helloooo. They go outside all the time. They roll around on the sidewalks, and yes, they are full of germs as my red, gooey eyes could attest. It took a full week for them to clear, and I was rinsing them constantly with every remedy I could get my hands on. It's your turn to be selfish and incredibly self-protective.

Seemingly harmless places such as pubs, restaurants, and even outdoor events can be treacherous terrain. The wind blows all kinds of germy things about. Bars and restaurants try to keep things clean, but how many times have you sat at a table and noticed they missed a few spots with their cold, wet rag? Other trouble spots are hand railings on stairwells and doorknobs, ATM keypads, and the list goes on and on. We shrug or turn a blind eye when we're strong because we know we can fight off those little, wimpy germs. Well, now you're the little wimp, and they're finally bigger and badder than you, and they're chomping at the bit to prove it. Don't give them the chance. The road is rough enough without having to add infection to the pile.

Another thing to avoid (and this is tough when your treatment moves through the holidays and other favorite events) are airplanes. They are the worst of the worst with all that recycled air, and if you think they wipe down all the seat arms and tray tables with antibacterial cleanser, then congratulations, your new name is Pollyanna~ It was my name when I decided to go against Dr. H.'s advice and go home for Thanksgiving. This was just barely two months into chemo. I figured I wasn't that far into it yet, and my white blood cell count (WBC) was just over the danger line before you have to endure the dreaded booster shot. Additionally I hadn't seen my family since I broke the news, and I felt compelled to put their minds at ease. Plus my sister puts on an amazing Thanksgiving feast every year, and I hated to miss it. I was still glad I went, but it came at a price. Just after I got back, there was blood in my urine, which they immediately tested and found a urinary tract infection. Ouch. It could've meant postponement of treatment, but it was an off week. There are different schedules for treatment I'm told, but mine was alternating one week on and one week off. So I went on antibiotics for a week, bought the local grocer out of cranberry juice, and swore never to ignore Dr. H.'s advice again.

Have I freaked you out yet? I hope not. There's no need to freak. You just need to see all this stuff with a new set of protective eyes to avoid these obstacles to your recovery. Wash all your fresh vegetables and fruits before eating them and keep a little bottle of that antibacterial stuff with you so you can wipe your hands wherever and whenever. When you're at a restaurant, go for the cooked stuff, and for fekssake, stop sharing forks, glasses, and the like with your loved ones. It's sweet, it's endearing, and it's just asking for trouble. Just think how much sweeter it will be when you're all done with treatment and headed into your new lease on life.

With all this hand washing and sanitizing, you can guess what else you need to stock up on: moisturizer, and get the good stuff. I actually used Neosporin for my fingertips because they seemed to get the worst of it. To each their own brand, but I like the moisturizers that smell like things I love. For example, I bought sugar scrub that smelled like fresh grapefruit and another that smelled like lemon. I also bought body cream that smelled like blueberries. Yummm. I put a little on my upper lip, especially when the chemical taste/smell invaded my sinuses. It was a nice little momentary reprieve.

Oh, they'll probably tell you this, but it bears mentioning here. They warned me to avoid manicures and pedicures. I didn't get it at first, but when you think about it, they often use sharp instruments that bore into the skin and expose it to all kinds of germs. All shops claim to be clean (and to the average eye they seem it), but they say it's not worth the risk. I had a regular manicurist because I'm useless at doing it myself, and I always end up with nail polish all over the place and me. I warned her of the risks, and she went into extra gentle mode with me, but again, ask your docs beforehand. They're the bosses of you.

While it's important to play it safe, pampering yourself is also really important. Whether you're a man, woman, or child, find whatever makes you happy. Maybe it's massage therapy, hydro therapy, or shopping therapy. If it is OK'd by the boss of you, go for it every chance you get. Just stay away from steam sauna...it sounds good, but it's not for you right now.

Well, now look at you...you've got all your questions answered, you are incredibly fearless, all your loved ones are in the know and clear on giving you what you need, your house and head are clean as a whistle, your medicine cabinet is filled to the brim, you've made a new, super laid-back friend, and you've got all you need to become a bona fide Germaphobe. Now it's time to head to the water.

———

Chapter 10:

HYDRATION IS THE NEW MANTRA

With so much of our bodies being made up of water, what's with the big push to drink at least a half-gallon of it every day? You'll actually notice it yourself if you don't follow this recommendation. I didn't. In fact, I stubbornly refused (ohhh, why must I always learn the hard way?) to take heed. You'll suddenly notice the back scratchers as you wait in line at the pharmacy and want to use them on your back that moment. Your hands and the skin around your feet and ankles will feel tight from the dryness, and then a light bulb will go off in your head.

There are two kinds of hydration you need. The first is in your hands. As in, you should be holding a bottle or tall glass of water right now. You're not? How 'bout you humor me and go do that now. It's ok, I'll wait. It's totally cool, I don't mind…
Some people buy it by the bottle or have it delivered. I think if I could go back, I'd have it delivered and keep a dispenser in the kitchen. It seems such an easy reminder to fill up each time you go in there. I fought this one tooth and nail because I'm almost never thirsty (unless a margarita is placed before me). So I felt as if I was forcing water down as a kind of punishment or something. I had the best intentions and bought a bunch of those reusable water bottles, but then I got wigged out over the germiness of them. Then I went for the twelve-pack of 32 oz bottles and added fresh lemon, lime, or unsweetened cranberry juice and pretended I was being très cool chick about it all. I kept a bottle on the bathroom counter to drink down the meds throughout the day and one by

my chair where I'd watch TV (my favorite escape) at night. That seemed to do the trick. Also the fear of another urinary tract infection helped. Since then, that large bottle of cranberry water is far more appealing. My latest kick is alkaline water. Look it up. It's supposed to be really good for detoxing your body. We have a massive supply in the town over, so I just go there once a week, rinse, and refill my three-gallon jug. Then I plop it back on its dispensing rack on the kitchen counter and voilà. It's very European, so of course, we (Americans who crave ties to our European heritage) are all into it.

The second is cellular. No, not the kind of cellular you ring up your friends on. It's the kind that is teeny tiny and fighting off those c cells. When you hydrate at the cellular level, you're making a big move in flushing those excess chemicals that have been pumped into your body all week out of your system. You don't want them piling up in there, trust me. Drinking water does this as well, so imagine how much faster you'll recover when you go for both. How does cellular hydration happen? Your nurse will ask you if you want it at the end of your chemo cycle and usually during. Again, every schedule is different, but after chemo, they'd offer to follow it up with hydration before I headed home. The following week, I'd come in for a blood draw (because they like to keep close tabs on your white blood cell count and be sure there are no infections going on in there), and they'd ask if I wanted to stay for hydration. I said "no, thanks" most of the time, and I'd be off on my merry way until I realized how much easier it would be to recover from a chemo cycle with it. Also, I had become really attached to my nurse mates and was never in a rush to leave.

For lack of a better place to put this note, I need to add how important it is to eat. I forget it doesn't come as easily to others as myself (mmmm...doughnuts), but when I hear about someone dropping down to eighty-five pounds, then I know I'm meant to say this. The docs and all can do their part, but you have to do yours, and a big part of your part is to nourish your body (whether you want to or not). Consume at least sixty grams of protein every day. Check with your doc for details on this, and whatever you do eat be sure to accompany it with your new love: agua.

How 'bout that now...you've got all your questions answered, you are obstinately fearless, all your loved ones are in the know and giving you what you need, your house and head are clean as a whistle, your medicine cabinet is filled to the brim, you've made a new, super laid-back friend, you've got all you need to become a bona fide germaphobe, and you're a veritable irrigation system. Are you feeling any better about all of this? Good, you should. Hopefully you'll do better with the next step than I did.

———

Chapter 11:

SWEAT LIKE A PIG

No, I'm not being a jerk. It's not the sweetest term, and it conjures up images that seem rather unpleasant, but this is just as important as the hydration mantra you've taken on. I'm living proof of how much longer it sucks when you don't. Just imagine all that water you're sucking down, that they're pumping into your body from the giant bag hung above you, and sloshing around with all those chemcials. Why aren't you peeing like a Russian racehorse? How are you going to push all that out? Some leaves on its own, but some just sits there (thanks to salt intake and plain stubbornness). So you need to give it a little push and they say sweating it out is one of the best ways to do it. My recommendation is to get on a stationary bike or rowing machine. Use something you can sit down on. This way, if you feel a bit light-headed, it's not too far to fall. The best time to go is straight from chemo on the day they unplug you or when you're done with the current cycle.

There's a bit of a high that happens when they unplug you, and you know you don't have to come back for x amount of days. A weight is lifted~ It's probably the most amount of energy you'll have for the next few days, so it's a great time to strike. I went back and forth on this one. It was much easier just to dress for the gym and go there directly. I live in the tiniest cottage on the planet, so fitting a bike in here would be, well…I'd have to also use it as my chair. Though there's really no room for a chair either, so…I did a lot of research and found a local gym. In many of the reviews, people mentioned "super clean," so I checked it out, and it was. They also had these hydro massage tables available, which is a great reward for working out. I was really tired by the time I started at the gym, so I began with twenty-five minutes and worked myself up to nearly an hour. Sometimes when I was feeling exceptionally energetic, I'd switch to the elliptical machine, but I'd stay away from anything that pounds the body such as aerobics or the running machine. Your bones are going through a beating already and are pretty fragile. Don't add to it. Like I said, I didn't follow this well-placed advice often, and I could always tell the difference.

The goal is to sweat from head to toe. The hair on the back of your neck should be dripping wet when you're done. Be sure to stretch before and after and…you guessed it: HYDRATE. Take at least a 32 oz bottle of water with you to the gym or your workout area at home, and it should be empty by the time you finish your workout. If you hate exercise (like me), then don't think of it as a weight thing. Think if you do it, you'll flush that crap out of your system sooner, and you'll be able to enjoy a marathon viewing of your favorite shows instead of curled up under the covers hoping (in vain) to sleep it off. The ideal thing would be to work out three days in a row after your chemo session which they call (how apropos) a "cycle". No worries if sometimes you aren't up for it. Don't push. Just don't waste that energy with a, "Hey, everyone. I feel great. Let's go out and eat, drink, and be merry tonight." I did that in the beginning because I was so determined to show my friends how tough I was. Each time I did, I woke up the next day feeling sick as a dog and flu-ish. I never said I was the smartest bird in the tree. When they told me I needed to do another three months of maintenance chemo, I saw it as a second chance to get it right. I've definitely stuck to my own exercise advice more this time (my friends are all shouting "LIAR" as they read this bit), but it was a struggle. I'm from a long line of couch potatoes who talk far more about what's for dinner than what's the best workout. Ah well, it's never too late to change, evolve, and break the chains that bind us to the past. Never~

Well, there you go…you've got all your questions answered, you are obstinately fearless, you've got all your loved ones in the know and waiting on you hand and foot, your house and head are spick-and-span, your medicine cabinet is bustin' out, you've made a new, super laid-back friend, you've got all you need to become a bona fide germaphobe, and you slosh as you walk you're so full of water. Even better, you have all the know-how on flushing this stuff out of your system between cycles. Are you feeling nice and full from this bounty of knowledge? Well, pat your belly and settle in 'cuz it's time to face one of the biggest stressors and break it down to a manageable size.

—

Chapter 12:

SHOW ME THE MONEY

This was probably the toughest one for me. Some have it tougher; some need not give it a thought. This chapter is dedicated to those whose hearts start to race every time they pull a bill out of the postbox and are slightly freaked at the thought of managing to pay for all this life-saving treatment and still keep a roof over their heads.

First, a note to those who don't have to give a thought to the money side. Have a think on this…there is no better time to stock up on those good karma points, and as you go through this course of treatment, you are going to witness loads of people who don't have it quite so good. No doubt, your money is your own, and you've earned every bit of it. Why should you give any of it to someone who didn't plan ahead or work as hard as you? You should because, even if you have the equivalent value of the crown jewels in your bank account, this ride will be a burden. The joy you can get from seeing relief on a stranger's face can easily increase those mighty mind and body-healing endorphins. Besides, doing good is, well, good. If I were in those shoes, I would want to give more directly than just to the cancer foundations out there (although, that is a great place to start). Donations have helped medical science make great strides in the search for a cure and in treatment.

Oh, if I could rule the world. I would donate anonymously to patients at the center in Secret Santa fashion. I'd first donate a yearly salary for a new position of patient advocate. This is one role most centers are sorely lacking, a financial and billing expert with an understanding and compassion for the situation. That person would sit down with the patients and spell out all the charges that were coming, what their insurance covered, and (if needed) a list of financial support resources. Then the patient advocate would help them fill out all the forms accurately, so they could take their stress about money down several notches and focus on getting well. "Stress less, heal more" is what the gal who helped me called it. Julie had the dream to start a foundation that does that and consults closely with all the cancer centers. I'd love to help make something like that happen. Obviously I haven't thought it through all the way, but you get the gist. You can make a huge difference in other peoples' lives while you're in the thick of it, and you can gain some of those endorphins everyone says are so good for you. Y'know, thinking on it further, I'd want to return to the hospital where I had all those surgeries I couldn't pay for. I'd sit down with the girls in the billing department and go through those delinquent accounts for people who didn't quite qualify for support. I'd help them pay off their accounts and give them my advocate's number to call whenever they came across a hard-luck case they couldn't help but wish they could. Yup, it makes me smile just thinking about it. As a matter of fact, if, by some stroke of luck, this book sells a million copies, then I may just do exactly that…so there.

I was lucky to find an independent, volunteer advocate like Julie, who helped me enormously. She told me about several local resources, went through my day-to-day expenses, and showed me where I could cut back (at least temporarily). In the end, she saved me a ton of money and stress. There was still a pile of bills, but at least it was a manageable one. Through those resources, I found reimbursement for gas/transportation, groceries, co-payments, and insurance premiums. Even with all the help though, you still have to pay attention. Chemo brain (we've discussed) meant I made more mistakes on forms and account updates than I can count. When that happens, be sure to whip out your c card.

Some people forget there's another human being on the other end of the line.

All said and done, my out-of-pocket expense has been about 30K, which is a lot to some and not much to others. For me it meant putting my dreams aside for now. There'll be more of that in the next chapter. I could fill a hundred pages with all the great things my friends and family did for me over the past year and a half (despite my resistance), but the important message you need to hear is that, when your friends and family volunteer to help you, say "THANK YOU." Know that by letting them help, you are helping them deal. Face it, oh defiant one, you need the help.

One example would be my sister, Shannon, insisted on coming down and "channeling Mom" while I had my surgery. She wouldn't take no for an answer, but we compromised, and she came as my sister and not my mom. Little did I know how much my sister and my mom had in common…as in, by the time I got back from the hospital, she had completely rearranged my kitchen and bathroom. As she was leaving, she pointed to my walk-in closet and said, "I didn't have time to get to that. Maybe next visit." She also went to the pharmacy and brought me back a bottle of much-needed painkillers and Red Vines (my fav) for my first night home. She even made her magic matzo soup and let me pick the movie for the night, so I'd say it was a banner week for us, and I am happy to admit to the world that, though we may not see eye-to-eye on some (OK, many) things, I love her to bits, and I know she loves me.

All my family and friends have been amazing, but I'm always afraid of accidentally leaving someone out. So I'll just say thanks for those times when you insisted I take a ride when I shouldn't be driving, you covered the rent when it was due, and there was only seven dollars in my account, you slipped your card to the waiter for countless meals where you refused to let me pay, you called me out when you thought I was doing something I really shouldn't, you knew I needed a moment of normalcy, you did handiwork around the house, and you pampered me when I didn't have the means or the mind to myself. You all know who you are, and to you, I say I love you, love you, love you. I am one of the luckiest people on the planet for having you in my life, and I remind myself of that every day.

You know...they say don't expect it, but I guarantee, if you allow it to happen when it comes your way, you will be surprised and touched by the generosity of others, and sometimes it's from those you'd least expect. OK, that's enough mush. Let's get back to your insider's guide~

A recap so far...you've got all your questions answered, you are oh so fearless, all your loved ones are baking, cleaning, and doing your paperwork, your medicine cabinet is a veritable pharmacy, you've made a new, super laid-back friend, you're a card-carrying germaphobe, and you're a veritable irrigation system that flushes between cycles. You've got some insider info on the money part of it (check the c card website for more resources). That should start to put your mind at ease if that's a stressor, and if not, I hope I've given you ideas on how to increase your health-improving endorphins while helping take the burden off others. Next we'll talk about something much more appealing.

———

Chapter 13:

DO WHAT YOU LOVE, AND THE HEALING WILL FOLLOW

❧ ❧ ❧

I'll bet you have started thinking about and possibly lamenting all the things you wanted to do in life and thought you had all the time in the world to do. Now you've started to wonder if you'll ever get the chance. This is another part of your whole new perception or outlook on life. That worry dissipates, and soon you'll start mapping out how and when to make one of those things on your bucket list happen. This is important. You need to have something to look forward to when the treatment is over, and you need to be able to visualize it. Imagine how you'll board that plane, get off at your long-awaited destination, and enjoy the trip all the more than you would've before when you were just taking life for granted or trudging your way through.

Even with all the financial help, I did have to put a lot of my dreams on the back burner. This included (my other passions are singing/songwriting and trying, but not really succeeding at playing guitar) recording a full-length CD. It also included long vacations with friends to Europe and Mexico. I dreamed of going to Isla Mujeres all last year. I was going to take half my tax return and set it aside for it. I was supposed to be finished with chemo (or so I thought) in the spring. I was going to give it two months for the sensitivity to sunlight to wear off, and then off I'd go to stroll the beaches, down some margaritas at the local cantina with my friends, and brave another fear by swimming with sharks. They'd be nurse sharks, of course, not the bitey kind. I am braver these days, but I'm not that brave. Not one to give up, I'm readjusting my vision of how these things are going to happen. Being cash poor has been a great lesson in frugality and how to be far more clever about money. Other things come first, and they may sidetrack your dates or the degree to which you'll afford to make that dream happen. You should, however, always have a plan for the future. Make a list of all the things you'd like to do and places you'd like to go, and start planning for them. Decide who you'd like to go with, and get them involved. Planning is half the fun, you know, and it's a great way to take your minds off darker matters.

As a matter of fact, get a pen, and write it down here and now. Go on. Write your top three. Write down what, where, with whom, and when. Maybe even include a ballpark figure of what you think it'll cost. This is your book. Don't you even think of lending or giving it to someone else. It'll be your memento of this time you're going through, and it'll be a great read later when you need reminding how far you've come, or in this case, where you're headed...

1.
What:
Where:
With Whom:
When:
How Much-ish:

2.
What:
Where:
With Whom:
When: How Much-ish:

3.
What:
Where:
With Whom:
When:
How Much-ish:

Hold onto those wishes, and make them known. It'll be fun to plan these trips out with whomever you want to go with, and it'll be a great break from your new routine. One of the great things (look, another silver lining) about going on medical leave (besides the much needed rest) is you'll have far more time than you'll know what to do with. I slept a lot and caught up on a lot of movies, but it also gave me time to work on my music, songwriting, and photography. I also did some in-depth planning on how to ease back into the work world with my newfound, far more creative skills. It also, of course, gave me time to write this book. I've been so excited about it I've been writing nonstop, and I finished the first draft within a week. I'm not good with sticking to any project long-term. I like ones that finish within ninety days or less. I get distracted so easily, which is a blessing and a curse. Getting distracted means I can be really annoying to myself and those who need me to remain focused, but it also means I am never bored~ I'll just focus on the silver lining of that one if you don't mind.

If this virtual c card brings you anything, I hope it acts as a constant reminder that you have earned the right to make it all about you right now. It truly is your turn to be selfish, regardless of what anyone says or does. It's going to be really difficult for those of you raised to put all others first. Parents especially will find this hard, but you must. There's no point in investing all this time, money, and energy into your treatment if you're not going to put yourself first. The docs and nurses can't do it all. You have to put your oar in as well and paddle. If it helps, think of it this way…you're not much use to anyone while you're sickly, so if you put all your best energy into yourself, you will heal more quickly and be ready to take care of them all again sooner rather than later…eh?

Part of putting yourself first means unapologetically choosing which social agendas to keep up with and which ones to drop for now (or for good). You can and should still do a lot of the things you enjoy in life. You just need to re-portion these activities to fit within your new schedule and energy reserve. Singing is definitely something I love to do. The week of chemo and the few days surrounding it, though, I couldn't. One of the side effects of my treatment was locked-up vocal cords, which made my throat feel kind of tight, and my voice sounded like it had a constant frogginess to it. That part of it is just post-nasal drip. How I hate most of the side effects. You're sitting there talking to someone, and then suddenly you're dripping away and frantically searching your purse for something to sop it up. This road ain't pretty. There are a lot of little embarrassing moments heading your way. Just take them in stride, and let yourself (and others) laugh through them when they happen. Be sure to surround yourself with people who can find the humor in it all. Humor is one of the mightiest of endorphin builders.

Remember, with chemo brain, you probably won't be able to handle intricate things. Your brain will just skip a beat here and there, and you'll find yourself lost in the middle of expressing a thought. I've actually blanked completely on new friends' names. The heart stays intact, though. I would beam at the site of them, but their names were just nowhere to be found. One friend's favorite was when I would space out while someone was talking to me or in the group, and then moments later, I would repeat what that person said as if it was my idea, only I couldn't remember how I got that idea. It drove her nuts. She spent more time with me than anyone during the course of it all. It wasn't that anyone else didn't want to. I just like to keep to myself a lot, and she's a nosey pants who panicked if she didn't hear directly from me that I was alive and well every couple of days. Once she'd confirmed I was alive and well, she went right back into piss 'n vinegar mode, but hey, sometimes those friends are exactly what you need to remind you that though you may be in a kind of social stasis, the rest of the world goes on...

I'd highly recommend getting really comfortable with your phone's calendar feature. It's a great tool for managing all the (now difficult to remember) appointment dates and times. If you have an old dinosaur of a phone, upgrade now. If possible, get a similar type. Nothing is worse than learning a new technology while all this is going on. I did, and I've worked in technology for over fifteen years. It didn't matter. With chemo brain, I felt like a primate trying to figure out the mysterious black, shiny thing. I used the calendar on my phone to remind me where I needed to be every day and when. I also used it to write notes to myself when I came up with an idea or an errand that needed to be carried out later. I'd sometimes forget details as I was typing in into the phone. It's the strangest feeling. I chose to make light of it. Most people went along, and when they didn't...I whipped out my c card as if to say, "Give me a fkn break, would ya? I'd like to see how well you'd do in this situation."

When it comes to this part of the guide, I don't think you need to write out your favorite things to do. Let it just come to you, and decide on the spot if you want to do something or not. Do NOT be afraid to disappoint others by canceling the day of or even an hour before. Your mood and energy levels will fluctuate without much notice. Learn to listen to your body, and give it precedence.

That was a hard one to learn for me. I hated missing out on all the fun and catching up. I'd get dressed up and mid-way through getting ready I'd start sweating. Then I'd look in the mirror, and I'd see this pasty gray, bloated face staring back at me. I looked like something on a morgue slab. I'd pout, then cry my eyes out for a bit while texting my cancellation, and then I'd shake it off, change into my super soft PJs, pour myself a big glass of bitter cranberry water, put on a funny movie, and all was right-ish with the world again. Always trust your instincts and your body.

How 'bout this for a recap...when you opened this book, your head was still reeling from the news. Now you've got all your questions answered, you are brilliantly fearless, all your loved ones are in the know and clear on giving you what you need, your house and head are clean as a whistle, your medicine cabinet is filled to the brim, you've made a new, super laid-back friend, you've got all you need to become a bona fide germaphobe, and you're a veritable irrigation system. Even better, you have all the know-how on flushing this stuff out of your system between cycles. You've got some insider info on the money part of it, and there are many more resources listed on the c card website. That should start to put your mind at ease if that's a stressor, and if not, you've been given some ideas on how to increase your health-improving endorphins while helping take the burden off of others. You've got at least three things to look forward to after the treatment is complete, and you can continue to do what you love (just in smaller doses). Feel free to explore new things that fit within your new schedule and fluctuating energy levels. Now it's time to wind up this insider's guide with a reminder of what you need to keep in the forefront of your mind at all times... YOU.

Never forget the importance of endorphins and what brings them on: exercising, laughing, smiling, flirting, hugging, being around people whose company you enjoy, doing social things you love, trying new things, giving yourself things to look forward to when it's over, and planning for them.

Remember, you've got a medicine cabinet that's chock-full, and don't you be afraid to use it. Stay on top of those symptoms. That's the trick. Take something the moment those symptoms come on. Once again, there are no guarantees for anyone on the outcome, but the road will definitely be much smoother for you if you follow these suggestions. Of that, I am living proof.

———

Chapter 14:

LETTER TO THE LOVED ONES

I know this is hard on you too. You want your loved one to get better ASAP. You're shocked at the realization that they may leave this world. You want to help, but you know there's such a fine line between helpful and overbearing. What can you do? How can you be most helpful? First and foremost is to remain calm. If you're freaked out, then it'll stress them out, and stress does NOT do a body good. If you read through the previous chapters you'll find all kinds of things you could help them out with.

Here's what I can tell you about most cancer patients. They are:

- Tired. Some days and moments in a day, they'll be too tired to cook, clean, keep up with the mail, or have conversations with anyone. Bringing them frozen meals is nice, but fresh is better since the microwave kills a lot of the nutrients in food. Think foods that are easy to digest, high in protein, and spicy. Everything smells and tastes weird to cancer patients, so avoid their favorite foods, or they'll risk hating them forever.
- Sick. Some days they may be too sick to get themselves to chemo treatment/hospital and back. So offers for rides are great.
- Cranky. They're going to have a significantly reduced tolerance for BS, so don't be surprised if they bite someone's head off for whining about Aunt Edna's backhanded compliments or whatever you two would normally go on for hours about in lively debate. On other days, though, they'll

crave to hear it all for the distraction. Be patient with your semi bi-polar buddy.

- Vulnerable. Their immune systems are compromised, so stay away if you have even the slightest cold. Passing that on could land them in the hospital. This is no joke. Also, if you bring them any raw foods, make sure they get washed with antibacterial soap before they eat them. Sushi (any raw meat) and grapefruit (in any form) are off-limits during treatment and until their doctor says so. Because they're so vulnerable, the best place for them is home most of the time. So don't suggest going out to bars or gyms or traveling of any kind while they're in treatment. They need to stay as protected as possible. However, they also need fresh air, so short walks (as long as they're protected from the sun) or bike rides will do them good.

- Proud. They may be too proud to tell you when they need something. Sometimes you may have to discreetly investigate to find their needs and fill them if you can. It's also very important you share that list of needs with others. Your c friend would never want to see you collapse from the weight of struggle to help them, and it's very important to set aside any differences with mutual friends/family. Conflicts only deplete what little energy they have.

- Sad. Even if they go on antidepressants, they will have sad moments. Let them have 'em, but don't let them feel too sorry for themselves. Remember the power of endorphins~

- Confused. Chemo brain is kind of like being stoned. Your otherwise bright friend will forget what he or she was saying mid-sentence, where keys were left, and (sigh) much, much more. Be kind, and don't expect that person to remember much of anything. Don't be offended if they forget plans or even put the wrong date and time in their calendar. This will last for at least a few months past treatment and then things will slowly go back to normal or at least closer to it. On that note, dealing with bills and paperwork (so much paperwork) can be really confusing, even without chemo brain. So if you're a whiz with numbers and navigating bureaucracy, then by all means, raise your hand for this assignment. They'll thank you later.

- Unattractive. This is worse for some more than others, but no one will feel like an amazing and alluring person. cancer patients are going through a serious ass whoopin', and it'll show. I don't care what they say. cancer is NOT sexy. They all can benefit from a little TLC, so if you have it in you to provide hair treatments, wigs, new hats, massages, or facials, they could all benefit from it. One of my favorites was a trip to the local day spa an herbal detox wrap at the end of a chemo cycle. Just remember to keep it to super clean environments for safety's sake. If you're not sure, just call the cancer treatment center, and they'll let you know.

- Slightly Deluded. They'll have days when they're feeling great and want to take it all on themselves. Knowing when to jump in and smack some sense into them is an acquired skill. My flying home that Thanksgiving probably should have been one of those times, but even more so was when I decided to take the coaster train from the airport back home. This involved bus rides and lugging stuff quite a ways. One of my equally obstinate friends got a hold of me shortly after landing and commanded I sit still and have her come down to pick me up. This is the hard part. People who are sick don't mean to question you per se. They just have those moments where they travel a little too far into denial city, and they need a little nudge back in the right direction.

The most important thing you can do is to NOT treat your friend like a dying person. Instead, carry on like that person is just going through a rough patch and needs some distraction and TLC, but no pity, like in a bad breakup. "That c punk is a loser, you're better off without 'em". Yeah, something like that. Your friend doesn't want to talk about cancer 24/7 and gets enough of that as it is. Don't try to control or nag either. They have very little control over their body or life right now, so sometimes he or she will want to exert the right to have a drink or go shopping at the mall. If they aren't keeling over, then let em have that moment of normalcy.

I remember midway through treatment, making plans to see Amos Lee in concert. I was so psyched. It wasn't a chemo week, so I thought I could get away with it. My two friends who were going with me asked a couple different times if I was sure I was up for it. I even offered to drive, but luckily they thwarted that and in a way that allowed me to keep my stubborn pride. I lasted only twenty minutes or so, and then it started…that feeling like all my energy was being pulled down out of my body. It's as if there's a magnet under the floor and your soles are being pulled down toward it. I spent the rest of the night on the stairwell of the venue because there wasn't any place to sit. I ruined their night out. I know it. I regret not paying more attention to my limitations. You will too, but these moments will happen, and everyone will learn from them. There's always hope.

———

EPILOGUE
When All Is Said and Done

❖ ❖ ❖

I wanted to close out this book on the highest note of all…when you've beaten this thing. You will be standing there thinking (at least, this is what I thought): well, this is rather anticlimactic, and don't I look like sht? Well, yes, but YOU MADE IT~ Yaaaay~ Celebrate in your favorite way, and then get yourself into recovery mode.

For each person, it'll be different, but one common requirement will be the need to detox. I'll be learning as I go along from here, but I'll be posting everything in blogs at TheCCardAndMe website to share with you all. I thought, however, I'd squeeze this one last story into the book before sending you off on your merry way. The center I went to offered a lot of complimentary services such as: Meditation, Acupuncture, Bio-feedback, Craniofacial Therapy, Music Therapy, Art Therapy, Reiki, Hypnotherapy, Massage, Pet Therapy, Qigong, and Yoga. They believed that integrating these therapies with traditional efforts was highly beneficial to the patient. I'm pretty middle of the road in my beliefs, but I knew it was important to keep an open mind and give some of them a try. I definitely recommend some of them if they're available to you. My nurses were strongly suggesting I explore Chinese medicine (namely acupuncture) to help kick-start my underactive thyroid (as it was already), but I hate needles, and I'm not that familiar with Chinese medicine, so I've been avoiding the pursuit (mostly because I haaaate needles).

Then one night, it came to me in a dream (no, really). I was being reintroduced to a guy I knew back in college (great guy, the kind you'd trust instantly, but I seriously hadn't thought of him in over twenty years) when I was studying theatre arts (one of many intended majors), and his name rang so loudly in my ears as I woke up that I had to look him up. It turns out Frank had moved on from the movie business, had gone into the field of medicine... Chinese to be exact, aaaand he and his wife have a place of practice just a couple hours away from me~ You can call it coincidence if you like, but really? C'mon...what are the odds? I sent him a note along with the odd story and (what, he can't think I'm a nutter, he's into Chinese medicine~) I heard back that same day. We recently met up for an appointment and so far so awesome. I didn't even flinch at the needles~. I'll blog about the experience on the c card website as we go along, so you're in the know. In the meantime, I read the detox page on their website and found that (surprise, surprise) a lot of the foods he recommends you consume during detox are the ones my body is craving anyway.

Foods to Include:

- Sea salt—helps accelerate the detox process
- Reishi mushrooms
- Kelp—seaweed products
- Miso soup—as in a macrobiotic diet
- Brown rice
- Green tea or black tea
- High carotene vegetables: yams, squash, carrots, Swiss chard, or spinach; orange and dark green foods: sweet potatoes, winter squash, beets, kale, collards, or chard

- Brassica vegetables (cabbage family): cabbage, broccoli, cauliflower, Brussels sprouts, arugula, turnips, radishes, mustard greens, or bok choy. These are particularly beneficial for their radio protective effects and ability to help repair radiation damage.
- High nucleotide content foods that assist in cellular repair: liver, sardines, mackerel, and anchovies
- Olive oil
- Beans and lentils
- Bananas—for potassium, if needed
- Water—consistently throughout the day

Foods to Avoid:

- Sweets—candy, soda, pastries, etc.
- Wheat and wheat products
- Limit alcohol and coffee intake

I don't know about you, but my arms cross in defiance every time I read the "Foods to Avoid" list. I know, I crave them toooo, ugh. Mostly, though, my body has been asking for green tea (sipping some now as I type), sea salt, Brussels sprouts, spinach, turnips (well...haggis, but turnips are always served with haggis), yams, beets, and cauliflower. I've also been craving my mom's age-old recipe for liver and onions, but I live in a tiny, duplex style cottage with a next door neighbor I like enough not to torture so, maybe best to wait on that one. Go ahead, look over the list yourself, and have a think on it...which of those listed foods have you been craving? Maybe you're more in tune with your body than you know...

Before we part, I'd like to take a moment to give a special thanks to friends and family who dug into their wallets and contributed to the campaign to ensure this book came to print. Words can't express my gratitude to all of you, but I'll start with an open acknowledgement of how awesome and inspiring you all are to me:

Gold Card-Carrying Members:

Bernadette O'Neill (in memory of her niece Jennifer O'Halloran and her mom Nora O'Neill), Christy Boles-Miedema (in memory of her mom Cindy Lu James), Debalou Riebe (in memory of her mom Karolyn Cavanaugh-Blank), Dianne Pollock (in memory of her father Jack Breheny), Hal Gilmore (in memory of my mom and his wife of nearly fifty years, Alice Gilmore), Ilene Robbins (in memory of her mother Elsie Robbins), Lisa Dujat (in memory of her friend Kymmie Bisnett), Margaret Lum (in memory of her dad Frank Lum "who loved Ali a ton"), Michelle Nelson (in honor of me 'cuz she's my BFF), and Pete Davidson (in honor of his mom, Joan, "who is doing just fine").

Platinum Card-Carrying Members:

Shannon Kahn (in memory of her sister-in-law Susan Kahn), and Steve Clare (in honor of me, "Da Baby").

I'd also like to take a moment to thank my team of medical geniuses without whom (though I'd love to take all the credit) I know I wouldn't be here to write this book. You know who you are and that you are all so amazing you'd make an atheist ponder the existence of angels.

This brings me to the next step up and onto the road to recovery. I'll be posting updates (for example, since this book first launched; Jen has earned the title of Registered Nurse. We call her "Jen RN" and couldn't be prouder) and what I learn as I go along at www.TheCCardAndMe.com. I encourage you to join in anytime and add your insights and experiences to them. There's an open comment section at the bottom of each page, so feel free. I love the thought of us all banding together to smooth the road ahead for others, don't you?

If you don't have cancer, just read this out of curiosity, then good for you for being pre-emptive. Doesn't it feel good to know now what to say and do whenever you do find out someone you know has cancer? Do me (and yourself) a big favor though will you, because it would mean a lot if you did. If you don't have any one of the following insurance policies in place; health, life, supplemental health and disability, go out and get them today, fer fkssake~ Chances are that one day even super-human you may be sick and it is so worth it to know that you won't have to worry about keeping that roof over your head, whether you can afford the best of care or even the gas to get there.

Last but definitely not least, if this book was helpful and you want to help pass it on, I won't mind one bit if you posted a positive review on Amazon.com and any of the other book review sites out there. Really, am totally good with it. I might even be grateful and do my silly, happy dance when I read it, 'cuz this is an Indie publication which means ehm, you are my publicist (streamers flying, crowds cheering), so from the bottom of my heart, thank you, thank you, you are the best publicist ever~

Now, on to the Road to Recovery. Hope to see you there~

———

Made in the USA
Charleston, SC
05 September 2013